# NEW HAMPSHIRE

## in words and pictures

**BY DENNIS B. FRADIN**

**ILLUSTRATIONS BY RICHARD WAHL**

**MAPS BY LEN W. MEENTS**

Consultant:
R. Stuart Wallace
Assistant Director-Editor
New Hampshire Historical Society

 CHILDRENS PRESS, CHICAGO

*For Richard, Carol and Lauren Bloom*

For their help, the author thanks:
R. Stuart Wallace, Assistant Director-Editor, New Hampshire Historical Society
David Starbuck, Archeologist, University of New Hampshire

Swift River

*Picture Acknowledgments*
NEW HAMPSHIRE DEPARTMENT OF RESOURCES AND ECONOMIC DEVELOPMENT—pages 10 (left), 16
GREATER MANCHESTER CHAMBER OF COMMERCE—pages 24(2), 25
WHITE MOUNTAIN ATTRACTIONS ASSOCIATION, INC.—pages 2, 10 (right), 19, 21, 22(2), 31 (top left & right), 32(2) 35(4), 37, 38, 43(2)
NEW HAMPSHIRE OFFICE OF VACATION TRAVEL—pages 4, 11, 14, 15, 17(2), 20(2), 26, 27, 28, 29, 30, 31 (left), 35 (bottom right), 36, 40

1 2 3 4 5 6 7 8 9 10 R 89 88 87 86 85 84 83 82 81

Library of Congress Cataloging in Publication Data

Fradin, Dennis B
New Hampshire in words and pictures.

SUMMARY: An introduction to the land, history, industries, cities, and famous sites and people of the Granite State.
1. New Hampshire—Juvenile literature. [1. New Hampshire] I. Wahl, Richard, 1939-    II. Meen Len W.    III. Title.
F34.3.F7         974.2         80-25421
ISBN 0-516-03929-6

New Hampshire

New Hampshire is a state in the northeastern United States. It is part of the area called *New England*.

New Hampshire is beautiful. It has forests where deer live. It has mountains where people ski and hike.

New Hampshire is also a very historic state. It was the first colony to form a government free of England. It was one of the original 13 states.

Do you know where President Franklin Pierce (PEERCE) was born? Or where Alan B. Shepard—the first American in space—was born? Do you know what state was hit by the strongest wind ever recorded?

You'll soon learn that the answer to all these questions is— the Granite State, New Hampshire!

New Hampshire gets very cold in the winter. But over a million years ago it was cold year-round. This was during the Ice Age. Huge sheets of ice, called *glaciers* (GLAY • sherz), covered the land.

The glaciers helped give New Hampshire the look it has today. They deepened valleys. These valleys later filled with water to become lakes. The glaciers also scattered rocks across the land.

Rocks and land formations found in the White Mountains

People first arrived in New Hampshire over 10,000 years ago. These people were hunters. They hunted deer and bears. The points they used on their hunting spears have been found. Their bone and stone tools have also been found.

In more recent times, two main tribes of Indians lived in New Hampshire. The Abnaki (ab • NAH • kee) Indians lived in the north. The Penacooks (PEN • ah • cooks) lived in the central and southern parts of New Hampshire.

The Indians fished with nets and spears. They hunted deer with bows and arrows. They grew corn.

The Indians lived in wigwams. These were huts made
of animal skins and tree bark. The Indians made canoes
for traveling on rivers. The tools and weapons they made
can be seen in New Hampshire museums.

No one knows who the first explorers in New
Hampshire were. Some think that Norsemen (men from
Norway) arrived about the year 1000.

In 1603 Martin Pring of England explored New Hampshire. Pring was looking for sassafras (SASS • ah • frass) trees. The bark of those trees was used in England for making tea. Pring is thought to have arrived at where Portsmouth (PORTS • muth) now stands. Another Englishman, Captain John Smith, explored the New Hampshire coast in 1614. Based on explorations by Englishmen, England claimed New Hampshire.

English settlers soon arrived. In 1623 David Thomson led settlers to where Rye now stands. They fished and traded with the Indians. At about this time Edward and William Hilton (HILL • tun) settled where Dover now stands. These first settlements were made near the Atlantic Ocean.

Cincinnati Hall, Governor's Lane, Exeter. The first section of this house was built in 1721.

In 1629 an Englishman named John Mason gained control of much of the area. It was granted to him by the English government. Mason named the land *New Hampshire* after his home county of Hampshire in England. Mason planned to bring settlers to New Hampshire.

English people came to farm and fish in New Hampshire. In 1630 the settlement that became Portsmouth was founded. In 1638 the towns of Exeter (EX • eh • ter) and Hampton (HAMP • tun) were founded.

In 1641 New Hampshire became part of Massachusetts. But in 1680 the king of England made New Hampshire a separate colony.

In the 1600s and 1700s many New Hampshire people farmed. First they cleared away forests. Then they planted corn, beans, and pumpkins. Sheep were raised for wool. The wool was made into clothes. The settlers raised cattle, chickens, and pigs. They also hunted deer and birds.

The Indians taught the settlers how to keep meat fresh by packing it with snow. They showed the settlers how to smoke meat. They also showed the settlers how to make medicines out of plants.

The covered bridge, the white frame church
(left) and the farmhouse (above) are typical of
New Hampshire.

When a new family moved into a town, they had to
build a house and "raise" a barn. Old settlers helped
them. When the work was done, everyone had fun.
People danced. They drank rum and cider. Some had
wrestling matches.

The settlers built churches and one-room schoolhouses.
Towns grew. Some people moved inland from the ocean.
By 1740 about 23,000 people had settled in New
Hampshire.

White Island, Isles of Shoals

People found other ways to make a living besides farming. Some chopped down trees. New Hampshire trees were sent to England where they were used as ships' masts. The trees were also made into ships in New Hampshire. Some New Hampshire people built shops inside or near their homes. Cloth, boots, and shoes were made in the shops.

Merchants sent New Hampshire products by ship to many countries of the world. The city of Portsmouth became home to many wealthy merchants.

From 1689 to 1763 England and France fought over lands in America. Many Indians sided with the French. They felt that the English had stolen their lands. New Hampshire men helped the English beat the French and the Indians in what are called the French and Indian Wars.

To pay for these wars, England placed high taxes on the American colonists. The colonists were ordered to pay taxes on tea and other products from England. The colonists were angry. They had helped the English beat the French and the Indians. All they got in return was more taxes.

Americans were also tired of being ruled by the king of England. They had built their farms and towns themselves. Now they wanted to rule themselves. Throughout the colonies, people spoke of forming their own country. New Hampshire was one of the first colonies to take action. In 1776 it became the first colony to form a government free of England.

The war to free the United States from England is called the Revolutionary War (rev • oh • LOO • shun • airy wore). A few rich New Hampshire landowners and merchants did not want to fight the English. But many New Hampshire men joined the fight. Some became "Minutemen." These were soldiers who could be ready to fight at a minute's warning.

Portrait
of General
John Stark

New Hampshire was the home of a famous
Revolutionary War general. His name was John Stark.
He had been born in Londonderry (LUN • dun • dairy),
New Hampshire. General Stark led Americans to a big
win near Bennington, Vermont, in 1777.

By 1783 the Americans had won the war. They were
free of England. The United States of America had been
born.

Stone barns, like this one near Lake Sunapee, were built to last.

New Hampshire became a state on June 21, 1788. It was the ninth state. In 1808 the city of Concord became the capital of New Hampshire. New Hampshire was nicknamed the *Granite State*. That was because hard rock called *granite* was mined there. Many fine buildings in the United States have been built from New Hampshire granite.

The people of New Hampshire were often said to be as "tough as granite," too. They had proven that when they broke away from England. They had proven it during long years of fighting the war. The state motto of New Hampshire shows the people's toughness and love of freedom. It is: *Live Free or Die.*

A metalsmith works at his craft.

In the early 1800s manufacturing (making things in factories) became important. Shoes were made in New Hampshire. In textile mills, cotton and wool cloth was made. In the city of Portsmouth alone, almost 500 ships were built between 1800 and 1850.

While ships made in New Hampshire took people across the seas, New Hampshire stagecoaches took people over the land. Since they were made in Concord, New Hampshire, they were called "Concord Stagecoaches." Sometime when you're watching a Western movie, you may see a Concord Stagecoach.

Above: Concord Coach
Left: Home of Franklin Pierce

New Hampshire produced a president, too, in 1853.
His name was Franklin Pierce. Pierce had been born in
Hillsboro, New Hampshire, in 1804. He went to school
and became a lawyer. When he was just 33 years old, he
was elected United States senator. Franklin Pierce was
only 48 years old when he became the president of the
United States. He served as president from 1853 to 1857.

While Pierce was president there was growing talk of
war in the United States. People in the North argued
with people in the South. Northerners spoke of ending
slavery. Many Southerners wanted to keep it. People
also argued about taxes and other issues.

The talking ended. Fighting began in 1861. This was the start of the Civil War. New Hampshire sided with the North. About 34,000 New Hampshire soldiers helped the North win the Civil War.

By the end of the Civil War, manufacturing was more important than farming. More and more factories were built. People from around the world came to work in New Hampshire factories. The cities grew bigger. Manchester (MAN • chess • ter) was already the state's biggest city, just as it is today.

During World War I ships were built near the city of Portsmouth. Submarines were built near that city during World War II. Shoes and uniforms were made in New Hampshire for soldiers during World War II.

Work for peace also occurred in the Granite State! Have you ever heard of the United Nations? It is a group of countries that works to keep world peace. In

Bretton Woods, in the White Mountains

1944 the International Monetary (MON • ih • tairy)
Conference was held at Bretton (BRET • un) Woods, in
New Hampshire. At this meeting, two United Nations
agencies were planned. One was the World Bank. It
provides money needed by some countries. The
International Monetary Fund was also formed. It helps
find ways for countries to trade with each other.

Hikers in the Presidential Range (above) and skiers on Wildcat Mountain (right) find much to do in New Hampshire no matter what the season.

A New Hampshire man named Alan B. Shepard, Jr., went far in 1961. Shephard had been born in East Derry (DAIR • ee), in 1923. He became a Navy pilot. Later he became one of the first astronauts. In 1961 Shepard became the first American in space. Ten years later, in 1971, he went even farther. He landed on the moon!

Back on Earth, many people discovered New Hampshire's beauty in the 1970s and 1980s. Tourism (the vacation business) became very important. Each year, millions of people visit the Granite State. They ski down its mountains. They visit its beaches that lie along the Atlantic Ocean. They hike through woods where Indians once lived.

20

You have learned about some of New Hampshire's history. Now it is time for a trip—in words and pictures—through the Granite State.

Pretend you're in an airplane high above New Hampshire. There are green forests almost everywhere you look. Almost 90 percent of New Hampshire is covered by forests. The state also has hundreds of sparkling blue lakes.

Lake Chocorua with Mount Chocorua in the background

Above: Winter in the White Mountains
Right: Travelers stop at an overlook on
Kancamagus Highway. This highway
runs through White Mountain
National Forest.

As you pass over the northern part of the state you'll see some lovely mountains. They are called the White Mountains. Do you see that huge body of water that touches the southeast edge of the state? That is the Atlantic Ocean. In the southern part of New Hampshire you'll also see the state's biggest cities—Manchester, Nashua (NASH • oo • ah), Concord, and Portsmouth.

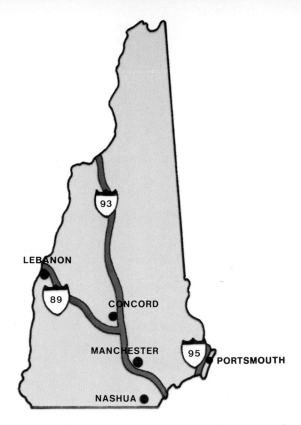

Your airplane is landing in a city near the state's southern edge. This is Nashua. It lies on the Merrimack (MAIR • ih • mack) River.

Settlers arrived here in 1660. The town that grew up here was named Nashua after an Indian tribe. Today, Nashua is the second biggest city in the state.

Furniture and shoes are made in Nashua. You might also have some Nashua products on your bed. Sheets and blankets are made in the city.

You'll enjoy the Arts and Science Center in Nashua. There you can see art works and learn about science.

Above: Manchester Institute of Arts and Sciences
Right: Manchester City Hall

If you follow the Merrimack River about 20 miles north of Nashua you will come to Manchester. Once, Penacook Indians lived here. Settlers arrived here from Massachusetts in 1722. Today, Manchester is the state's biggest city.

Visit the Currier (CUR • ee • er) Gallery of Art in Manchester. You'll see many famous paintings there. If you want to see some more art works, go to the Manchester Institute of Arts and Sciences.

You'll enjoy the John Stark house in Manchester. American Revolutionary War hero John Stark lived there.

The people who live in Manchester today are interesting, too! You may notice that many speak French. Their grandparents and great-grandparents were French-speaking Canadians. There are many people of Canadian background in New Hampshire.

The people of Manchester work at many jobs. Some make shoes. Clothes and computer equipment are just two other products made in the state's biggest city. Manchester products are sent to many other cities in the United States.

Greater Manchester Chamber of Commerce

Commercial fishing boats in Portsmouth Harbor

From Manchester, head east towards the Atlantic Ocean. Then take a trip up New Hampshire's 18-mile Atlantic Coast. You'll see fishing boats off the coast. Lobsters, cod, shrimp, and flounder are four of the seafoods caught in coastal waters. You'll see lighthouses that guide boats to shore. The coast also has beaches where people swim and sun themselves.

The city of Portsmouth lies where the Piscataqua (pis • CAT • ah • kwah) River flows into the Atlantic Ocean, in southeastern New Hampshire. Portsmouth is a very old city. It was founded in 1630. It was called Strawbery Banke at first, because of the wild strawberries that grew there.

Jackson House, Portsmouth, was built in 1664.

Visit Strawbery Banke in Portsmouth. In this area of Portsmouth you can see what the settlement looked like back in the 1700s.

There are many old buildings and houses in Portsmouth. The Moffatt-Ladd (MOFF • it • LAD) House was built in 1763. William Whipple once lived there. He signed the Declaration of Independence. The Governor John Wentworth House was also built in 1763. Wentworth was an English governor. He was run out of town by a group of Americans in 1775, just after the Revolutionary War began!

John Paul Jones House, Portsmouth

Did you ever hear of John Paul Jones? He was a great naval hero who is called the *Father of the American Navy.* If you visit the John Paul Jones House in Portsmouth you can see where he once lived.

Today, the Portsmouth Naval Shipyard and the Pease Air Force Base are both near Portsmouth.

Dover is just 12 miles northwest of Portsmouth. Dover is another very old city. It was first settled in the 1620s. Boats, electric motors, machinery, and shoes are made in Dover today. You'll enjoy the Damm Garrison in Dover. It is a log cabin that was built in 1675.

State capitol

About 40 miles west of Dover you will come to the city of Concord. It lies on the Merrimack River. Concord was founded in 1727. It has been the capital of New Hampshire since 1808.

Visit the state capitol building. Lawmakers from all over New Hampshire meet there. You can watch them as they work on laws for the Granite State. In recent years they have worked on laws to improve the state's schools. They have worked on laws to clean up the state's rivers and lakes. They have worked to improve the lives of old people.

Would you like to see where a president lived? Visit the home of Franklin Pierce in Concord. Our 14th president lived here from 1857 to 1869.

You'll see some farms near Concord and in many areas of southern New Hampshire. Farming isn't very big in the state today. But farmers do raise potatoes, corn, apples, grapes, and other crops. Some farmers raise milk cows. Others raise beef cattle. Sheep, turkeys, chickens, and eggs are other farm products.

Cattle graze in Jefferson Meadows. The Presidential Range is in the background

Farms (above) and stone walls (left) are found throughout the state.

New Hampshire farms are lovely. On some farms, you will see stone walls. You remember that, long ago, glaciers dropped rocks across the land. Farmers had to move those rocks. They didn't let the rocks go to waste. They built stone walls out of them. The walls fenced in farm animals.

Without a doubt, the brilliant fall colors make the state a tourists' delight.

The small towns in farm areas are pretty, too. You can still see some old one-room schoolhouses. You can see lovely old churches. You can see covered bridges once traveled by Concord Stagecoaches.

North of Concord you'll come to an area known as New Hampshire's "Lakes Region." It has lovely rolling hills and beautiful lakes. In the fall, the trees in this area blaze with color. The gold, orange, and red trees next to the blue lakes are beautiful. Artists come to this area to paint pictures.

Visit Lake Winnipesaukee (win • ih • pih • SOCK • ee), which is the state's largest lake. Indian tools dating back over 9,000 years have been found there. At a later time, a big Indian village was located on the lake.

According to one Indian story, a man and a woman from two enemy tribes got married. After the marriage, the couple paddled their canoe across this lake. The Indians felt that this marriage would make their great god happy. So the Indians named the lake *Winnipesaukee*—meaning "the smile of the Great Spirit."

North of the Lakes Region the hills turn into mountains. You have entered the White Mountains. The rocky tops of the mountains look white in the sunlight. That is probably how the White Mountains got their name. But in the summer, trees turn the White Mountains almost solid green.

In the winter, however, the White Mountains really do look white! They are covered by snow. Then, people head into the White Mountains to ski and snowmobile.

You'll enjoy Cannon Mountain in the White Mountains. A huge rock on Cannon Mountain is called the *Old Man of the Mountain.* Can you tell why? This granite rock really does look like an old man's head. The Old Man of the Mountain is a famous New Hampshire landmark.

You can ride to the top of Cannon Mountain on a tramway. There is a fire tower on top of Cannon Mountain. From there, rangers watch for fires. The beautiful forests that cover the mountains are valuable. They are used for making paper and lumber.

The Flume (FLOOM) is very near the Old Man of the Mountain. The Flume is a narrow canyon. It was carved by water over many years. You'll see pretty rocks in the Flume. You'll see waterfalls. You can walk through the Flume on a specially-built path.

Visitors to the White Mountains can walk through the Flume (top left), hike on Cannon Cliff (middle left), ski on Cannon Mountain (bottom left), walk across Sentinel Bridge and Pool, the Flume (top right), and take pictures of Old Man of the Mountain (bottom right).

Mount Washington Hotel in the Presidential Range

The Old Man of the Mountain and the Flume are both in a wide gap between two mountain ranges. This gap is known as Franconia Notch (fran • CONE • eeya notch).

One mountain range in the White Mountains is called the Presidential Range. It has mountain peaks named after presidents. You'll see Mount Adams, Mount Jefferson, Mount Monroe, Mount Madison, Mount Eisenhower (EYE • zen • how • er), and Mount Washington there. At 6,288 feet, Mount Washington is the tallest point in the state. It is also the tallest peak in all of the northeastern United States.

Cog train on Jacob's Ladder, Mount Washington

You can take a train to the top of Mount Washington.
The little train is called the Mount Washington Cog
Railway. Mount Washington can get very windy. The
strongest wind ever measured on Earth hit Mount
Washington, in 1934. The wind reached the speed of 231
miles per hour. That's much stronger than a hurricane!

People aren't the only ones who enjoy the White Mountains. Many animals live there. Beavers build their dams in the woodland streams. Chipmunks dart through the forests. You can see deer and foxes. Raccoons, rabbits, and porcupines can also be found. If you see a black and white animal with a bushy tail and a cute little face, don't pet it. It's a skunk. Skunks can be seen—and smelled—in New Hampshire.

The White Mountains stretch into the far northern part of New Hampshire. You may feel it getting colder the farther north you go. In the winter, it can be -15° or colder in far northern New Hampshire. In 1925 the temperature dipped to -46° in the state's northern tip. That's New Hampshire's record low temperature.

Plowed road in the White Mountains

Paper companies own timberland in far northern New Hampshire. But there are few roads and towns here. The land looks much as it did when only Indians and fur trappers were there.

The northern edge of New Hampshire lies along the border with Canada. The far northern part of New Hampshire was once claimed by *both* the United States and Canada. The people who lived there decided they didn't want to be part of either country. They formed their own country, called the Indian Stream Republic. In 1842, however, by the Webster-Ashburton Treaty, the area was made part of the United States. A historical marker in Pittsburg, New Hampshire, tells you about the short-lived Indian Stream Republic.

Places don't tell the whole story of New Hampshire. Many interesting people have lived in the Granite State.

Birthplace of Daniel Webster

Daniel Webster (1782-1852) was born in Salisbury (SAULZ • bury), New Hampshire. He went to the famous Dartmouth (DART • muth) College in Hanover, New Hampshire. Webster became a lawyer and a famous speaker. As a United States senator, he tried to help America avoid the Civil War. As the Secretary of State, he helped make the Webster-Ashburton Treaty. This settled the argument over the land that lies along the United States-Canada border. You can visit the Daniel Webster Birthplace, near Salisbury.

Salmon Portland Chase (1808-1873) was born in Cornish, New Hampshire. He became a lawyer. Chase hated slavery. He defended runaway slaves in court. As a United States senator, Chase tried to stop the spread of slavery in the United States. Did you ever hear of the Supreme Court? It is the highest court in the United States. Salmon Portland Chase was Chief Justice of the Supreme Court from 1864 to 1873. Another New Hampshire man, Harlan Fiske Stone, served as the chief justice from 1941 to 1946.

Henry Wilson (1812-1875) was born in Farmington, New Hampshire. He was very poor. He didn't get to go to school very long. But Wilson loved to read. He taught himself many subjects. As an adult, Henry Wilson entered politics. He helped found the Republican Party, which opposed slavery. Henry Wilson served as the 18th vice-president of the United States from 1873 to 1875.

Horace Greeley (1811-1872) was born near Amherst, New Hampshire. Greeley became a printer. He started his own newspaper, the *New York Tribune*. Greeley believed that the western part of the United States had a great future. "Go West, young man," he said. Greeley followed his own advice. He founded the town of Greeley, Colorado.

Mary Baker Eddy (1821-1910) was born in Bow, New Hampshire. She grew up on a farm. Mary Baker Eddy was once badly injured. She believed she was healed through prayer. After that, Mary Baker Eddy founded a new religion. It is called Christian Science.

Daniel Chester French (1850-1931) was born in Exeter, New Hampshire. He became a sculptor. When he was just 23 years old he made a statue of an American Revolutionary War soldier. This well-known statue is called *The Minute Man*. French also made the statue of Abraham Lincoln at the Lincoln Memorial in Washington, D.C. That is one of the most famous statues in the United States.

Above: Highway through Crawford Notch
Right: Sabaday Falls, White Mountains.

Robert Frost (1874-1963) was born in California. But he lived for many years in New Hampshire. Frost was a poet. He wrote about country life in New Hampshire and Vermont. "After Apple-Picking" and "Birches" are two poems by this great writer.

Home to President Franklin Pierce ... Daniel Webster ... astronaut Alan B. Shepard ... and Mary Baker Eddy.

A land of forests ... mountains ... seashore ... and sparkling lakes.

A state where you can see pretty farms ... old buildings ... and The Old Man of the Mountain.

This is New Hampshire—the Granite State!

## Facts About NEW HAMPSHIRE

Area—9,304 square miles (44th biggest state)

Greatest Distance North to South—180 miles

Greatest Distance East to West—93 miles

Borders—Canada to the north; Maine and the Atlantic Ocean to the east; Massachusetts to the south; Vermont to the west

Highest Point—6,288 feet above sea level (Mount Washington)

Lowest Point—Sea level, along the Atlantic Coast

Hottest Recorded Temperature—106° (at Nashua, on the Fourth of July in 1911)

Coldest Recorded Temperature—Minus 46° (at Pittsburg, on January 28, 1925)

Statehood—Our ninth state, on June 21, 1788

Origin of Name New Hampshire—New Hampshire was named for the county of Hampshire, in England; that was the home county of John Mason, an early New Hampshire landowner

Capital—Concord

Counties—10

U.S. Senators—2

U.S. Representatives—2

State Senators—24

State Representatives—400

State Songs—"Old New Hampshire," "New Hampshire, My New Hampshire," and "New Hampshire Hills"

State Motto—*Live Free or Die*

Nickname—The Granite State

State Flag—Adopted in 1909

State Seal—Present one was adopted in 1931

State Flower—Purple lilac

State Bird—Purple finch

State Tree—White birch

44

Some Rivers—Connecticut, Ammonoosuc, Sugar, Mascoma, Ashuelot, Androscoggin, Merrimack, Nashua, Saco, Piscataqua

Lakes—About 1,300 (the largest is Lake Winnipesaukee)

National Forest—White Mountain National Forest

State Parks—34

State Forests—103

Animals—Deer, foxes, rabbits, beavers, raccoons, chipmunks, otters, porcupines, skunks, ducks, geese, pheasants, grouse, sea gulls, many other kinds of birds, snapping turtles and other turtles, rattlesnakes, and other snakes, many kinds of frogs and toads

Fishing—Lobsters, cod, haddock, flounder, shrimp, smelt

Farm Products—Milk, chickens, turkeys, eggs, beef cattle, apples, peaches, strawberries, blueberries, grapes, potatoes, corn, hay, maple syrup and other maple products

Mining—Sand, gravel, granite, quartz, garnets, mica, feldspar

Manufacturing Products—Electrical equipment, machinery, paper and wood products, leather products including boots and shoes, metal products, food products

Population—849,000 (1977 estimate)

Major Cities—
| | | |
|---|---|---|
| Manchester | 80,900 | (all 1979 estimates) |
| Nashua | 66,400 | |
| Concord | 28,800 | |
| Portsmouth | 24,300 | |
| Dover | 21,400 | |
| Keene | 21,100 | |
| Rochester | 21,100 | |

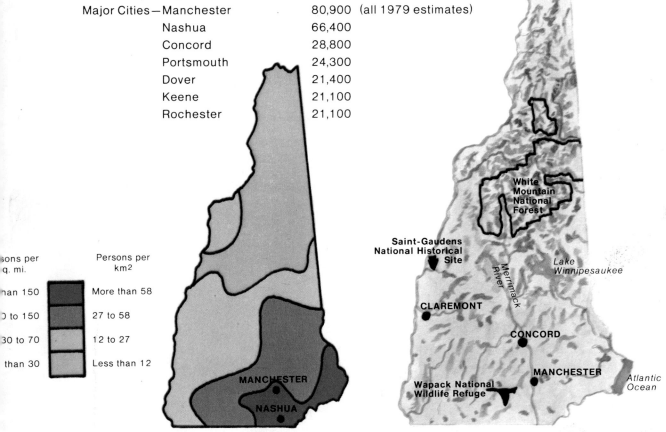

sons per
q. mi.

Persons per km2

han 150 — More than 58

0 to 150 — 27 to 58

30 to 70 — 12 to 27

than 30 — Less than 12

MANCHESTER

NASHUA

Saint-Gaudens National Historical Site

White Mountain National Forest

CLAREMONT

Merrimack River

Lake Winnipesaukee

CONCORD

MANCHESTER

Atlantic Ocean

Wapack National Wildlife Refuge

# New Hampshire History

There were people in New Hampshire at least 10,000 years ago.

1603—Martin Pring of England is the first known explorer in New Hampshire

1614—Captain John Smith explores the Isles of Shoals

1623—David Thomson makes a settlement at Rye; Edward Hilton settles at Dover at about this same time

1629—Englishman John Mason receives a large amount of land and names the area *New Hampshire*

1630—Portsmouth (called Strawbery Banke at the time) is founded

1641—New Hampshire becomes part of Massachusetts

1680—The king of England makes New Hampshire a colony

1727—Concord is settled

1740—Population of the New Hampshire colony is about 23,000

1756—New Hampshire's first newspaper, the *New Hampshire Gazette,* is published at Portsmouth

1763—After almost 100 years of fighting, the French and Indian Wars end with England winning; to pay for these wars, England puts heavy taxes on the American colonists

1769—Dartmouth College is founded

1775—John Wentworth, the English governor of New Hampshire, is driven out; in this same year the Revolutionary War begins

1776—New Hampshire becomes the first colony to form a government free of England

1783—Thousands of New Hampshire men have helped the United States win the Revolutionary War

1788—On June 21, New Hampshire becomes the ninth state

1800—Population of the state is 183,868

1805—The Old Man of the Mountain is discovered

1808—Concord becomes the state's permanent capital

1832—Indian Stream Republic is formed in northern New Hampshire during a border dispute between the United States and Canada

1838—Railroad first enters state

1842—Webster-Ashburton Treaty settles border dispute with Canada

1853—Franklin Pierce, born in Hillsboro, becomes the 14th President

1861-1865—About 34,000 New Hampshire men help the North win the Civil War

1869—Railroad to the top of Mount Washington opens

1900—Population of the Granite State reaches 411,588

1911—White Mountains area becomes a national forest

1917-1918—After the United States enters World War I, over 20,000 of the state's people are in uniform; ships for the war effort are built at Portsmouth

1919—State Board of Education is organized

1934—On April 12, winds reaching 231 miles per hour hit Mount Washington; this is the strongest wind ever measured on Earth

1936—Floods hit state

1938—Hurricane hits state

1941-1945—After the United States enters World War II, over 60,000 New
Hampshire men and women are in service; submarines are built
at Portsmouth

1944—During the war, the International Monetary Conference is held at Bretton
Woods

1959—Kancamagus Highway, going through the White Mountains, opens

1961—Alan B. Shepard, Jr., born in East Derry, becomes the first American in
space

1964—The New Hampshire sweepstakes lottery begins, with the proceeds
helping to finance public education

1970—State adopts a tax on business profits

1979—Hugh Gallen becomes the governor

# INDEX

47

## INDEX, Cont'd

About the Author:

Dennis Fradin attended Northwestern University on a creative writing scholarship and graduated in 1967. While still at Northwestern, he published his first stories in *Ingenue* magazine and also won a prize in *Seventeen's* short story competition. A prolific writer, Dennis Fradin has been regularly publishing stories in such diverse places as *The Saturday Evening Post, Scholastic, National Humane Review, Midwest,* and *The Teaching Paper.* He has also scripted several educational films. Since 1970 he has taught second grade reading in a Chicago school—a rewarding job, which, the author says, "provides a captive audience on whom I test my children's stories." Married and the father of three children, Dennis Fradin spends his free time with his family or playing a myriad of sports and games with his childhood chums.

About the Artists:

Len Meents studied painting and drawing at Southern Illinois University and after graduation in 1969 he moved to Chicago. Mr. Meents works full time as a painter and illustrator. He and his wife and child currently make their home in LaGrange, Illinois.

Richard Wahl, graduate of the Art Center College of Design in Los Angeles, has illustrated a number of magazine articles and booklets. He is a skilled artist and photographer who advocates realistic interpretations of his subjects. He lives with his wife and two sons in Libertyville, Illinois.